The Other Hemisphere

Poems by Jan Kemp

Three Continents Press

Second printing 1992

Three Continents Press
1901 Pennsylvania Avenue, N.W.
Washington, D.C. 20006 USA

ISBN: 0-89410-716-X (cloth)
ISBN: 0-89410-717-8 (paper)

Library of Congress Number: 91-065185

Published in Australia by Butterfly Books
P.O. Box 107; Springwood, NSW 2777

Distributed in New Zealand by Brick Row Publishing Co. Ltd.
P.O. Box 100-057; Auckland 10

Cover etching, "Hibiscus Still Life," by Claudia Pond Eyley

Calligraphy by Jan Kemp
Design and typesetting by Norman Ware
Back-cover photograph by Reginald Hunt

Printed in Singapore
by General Printing Services Pte. Ltd.

The Other Hemisphere

to my mother
to the memory of my father
& to Goh Poh Seng
with love

Acknowledgements are due to publications in which some of these poems first appeared: *Landfall*, *The N.Z. Listener*, *Westerly*, *Kunapipi*, *An Anthology of Twentieth Century New Zealand Poetry* (Oxford University Press, 1987) and *Five Poems* (Arte & Materia 1988, Singapore). "Anawhata Sequence" first appeared in *Kiwi & Emu: An Anthology of Contemporary Poetry by Australian and New Zealand Women* (Butterfly Books, New South Wales, 1989).

"At Telegraph Bay" and "Junks" from "Seascapes, Hong Kong," together with three poems by John Spencer have been set to music by Australian composer Anne Boyd in *At Telegraph Bay: Five Songs for Baritone with Piano* (Faber Music, 1983); the poem sequence "The Other Hemisphere" was first presented at the multi-media exhibition, Arte & Materia 1990, National Museum Art Gallery, Singapore, in calligraphy and as a cassette recording in Aldo Fregado's installation "The Poem Tree."

Contents

The Other Hemisphere

In the other hemisphere Rilke speaks of,
best known to poets and woman whose
unattainable love lives in her mind,
a ghost seen always at his most beautiful,
so gentle he holds her like air, showing
the fullness of heaven by not being there;

deliberately hidden, yet discovered
years after, suddenly in her mind's eye
on the way to the airport, perhaps,
from the backseat of a taxi, one in a stream
cruising by as shiny and black
as patent leather, seductive as tuxedos,

the thought of him only
rises, flawless as emptiness,
whose wingspan tips the horizon's edges
acknowledging her solitude,
what is left by his absence
filling her sky.

Into
That
Space

Into That Space

for Charles Causley

Into that space
behind my eyes
my mind's clerestory
I come walking
the grassed nave of the sky's abbey
at sunset
when all of England
goes round and round
like black-faced sheep on a tor
like blood-springs
of red valerian
flaring round and round
ruined walls
up into the dark.

Is this
where I must go alone
can you not come with me
who showed me
the incredible Magdalene's
supine back
her unguent bowl like her hair
carved on a granite church
her back
curved forever beside
where we tossed pebbles up
to keep Celtic luck
will you not come my friend
who showed me St Juliot church & stream

where ragged robins
overrun the Vallency Valley
and Thomas met Emma.
Can we not go together, slip away
just us, while time's ripe?
No one will notice
go where poets go and be always
driving around in the English language
somewhere like Cornwall
in a clutch-ridden car
stalling at fords
dining at *The White Hart*
the pure burning white-heated
heart of poetry?

Angelic encounters
have the life-span of candles
yet stay held
in the spine's hollow
rising like *kundalini* to the mind
your voice honing my ear
your sight opening my eyes
as you heard me
taught me
showed me the way
out of earth's crypt
to the singing path
up through the invisible
vaultings of the dark.

Chagall Windows, Fraumünster, Zürich

for my mother, May 10th, 1987

I

Figures in blue glass, yellow glass, red glass
fall through shafted sunlight like voices pitched beyond
ear-pitch, tumbling into sound.

Staining the air
they leap and hover
free-flying as prisms.

The ear's eye, eye's ear follow them
together, *zusammen*, two senses
acrobatic as bodies, loving,

while each yet curves its lineage.
The voices cross and kiss
in slow polyphony as they pass

those long narrow beds of light
letting the invisible into the morning chapel
through warmed walls of stone.

Which one mind conceived
Mozart's "Great Mass"? So attuned
it plunged through his ears like light

patterning the stainings in the glass
with kyries, with glorias. Beneath the windows
Zürich *Frauen* fuss over table-cloths, the morning-tea

as in the cathedral the choir rehearses.
A solo soprano wanders an exultant way
above the organ loft.

II

A child signed with water at the font is folded
into the family—God is *Gott*, children *Kinder*
in this foreign, not unfamiliar tongue.

My first day in Europe I have gate-crashed a Baptism
slipped in at the wrong end of the church.
They smile, make room for me.

I sing from a Waikato childhood's stainings
early Communion and Evensong on Sundays
a hemisphere and thirty years away.

The soprano lifts the roof.
Chagall floats in through the great rose window.
Mozart somersaults the colours. It is Mothers' Day.

At Glastonbury Abbey

The journey's gypsy draws you on
with sounds of silver: double-images
hallucinate from a stone. The face
of a girl, where? Is she here?
There? A monk's sandal, did you hear him
pass on the quick, soft grass?

Sun-warmed ceramics lie patterned
in a floor-tile patch
an eagle rampant, a starfish
stranded in a walkway
aisled by fern-leafed beech trees
swimming in summer's air.

Adrenalin pricks without touch.
Your mind spins over the lawn
beneath the crowned ropings
of Joseph's staff turned thorn.
Arimathea carried that as
Christ lugged crossed beams.

This is England and there
Guinevere's hair's found coiled
there lies Arthur's head. We are,
they exist. No-one is dead.
The nave's grasses grow
into broken cathedral vaultings

triple-arching the madonna blue
catapulting earth into space.
If, cupped in life's palm, human days

were gentle, true and kind,
you'd find grail on the wind
like manna or white daisies, lasting, lasting.

At Stonehenge

In my favourite Stonehenge photograph
they're all running away out of the rain
singly or in tandem, balancing their stone
hats and umbrellas
                                        after tourists
at a clip for the Frames Rickards coach
careful not to spill styrofoam cups of carpark
canteen coffee from across the highway.
Warm and dry again in the bus the tour guide

reassures everyone, *it's best* (hence the roped
enclosure) *the stones aren't touched don't have
slogans or graffiti spray-painted on.
Their bodies*, she explains
                                                    *wear away under
modern sand-blast-cleaning techniques.*
The tourists nod solemnly. The stones quietly
sip coffee enjoying the human contact.
Besides, there'd be nothing to visit

*no perpetuity to awe us, no measure against
our own poor, forked . . .* Overwhelmed, she sits.
No jobs for tour-guides, no tourists? The sarsen
in the next seat turns, tips his lintel and smiles.

Sunday Morning in Kent

for Nizametdin Akhmetov

So much bird-song, church bells,
& the trees still uprooted from that storm.
Sunday morning in Kent; as I walk out of the woods,
the rector walks down from the rectory.

To be free in the mind, just to write, Niza;
the hope of clarity for each to focus with,
as after sleep, instead of stumbling about,
insomniac, in the undergrowth.

How did you keep yourself while they ravaged you,
those twenty years inside? Did you hear again the muezzin
& the birds you'd heard, the twenty years before,
a village boy from Kunashak, near Chelyabinsk?

Nizametdin Akhmetov, who first protested on behalf of minority groups in the Soviet Union, started to write while spending twenty years in Soviet prisons and mental hospitals until his release, at age 39, in 1987, after his case was taken up by many, including International PEN. He lived in West Germany and published *Die Strasse der Freiheit* (Fischer Verlag, 1988), and in 1990 returned to Russia.

Looking at St. Paul's

Today we both wear
purple on the skin
regal, ethereal
lifted to an inner sky
from a mutual bed, our eyes
glazed with the stains
of love's windows.

You see spires
I, domes;
you plunge fathoms
I rise around you,
we swell as sea-flowers.
Across the Thames
cranes shift and swing

lift and dump bits of London
behind the perfect cupola.
We are seagulls
endlessly
turning up-river
down-river.
Now you've gone.

My tongue floats alone
in its mouth cradle. The after-image,
your head lolling in my thighs,
recalls that flash,
sun on river
through high windows,
once, always, never, ever.

You Hoped It Is Love In Your House

for Anna in Basel

Not only love, love distilled
springs in the acacia, where the mind's winter birds
wake to parties in summer gardens;
goldfish breed in the daisies
& a rabbit swims through uncut grasses.

The sun's steep over the roof way down under
from where the moon's come
so quickly up a hemisphere.
She moves bellyful through the wheatfields.
Did anyone ever name her quite rightly?
She's a swan.

Schubert swells in every room
where each can return to self.
A bubbling in the ventricles
blood of the lamb, some call it
that wine at meeting, at parting.
At home, *arohanui*, great love

we now say, for what the birds tune to
remind us we and they are made of, we turn to.

A Grim Tale

Strewelpeter plays
classical trumpet in the *Schwarzwald*
warped boy
his fingernails
strut sharply on the keys.

Schmerz emerges.
Alas, the pain! cry the haut-boys
in the pews of the accompanying keys.

Aue, Aue! cry the ozoned trees
schizoid in the green/brown
Schwarzwald forests.

Strewelpeter writhes
in a subterranean basement, his snake-
like trumpet pulsates.

He hates bodies, the flesh, summer
& sun-bathers. His trumpet
is the sublimated gold

of his spot-lit virginity.
He hates the kiss-cheek women
at house concerts. At night

he clips his nails, fondles
the trumpet in a bed of wild flowers
and his heart explodes with music.

There is a price for talent.

Strewelpeter flicks his black
coat-tails, slips past the table-cloth
the prize embossed pewter goblets

cringes at the adoring girls
and slides into strange relations
with the married *Frau* next door.

There is a grand piano in her practice room.
He uses her without thinking. She might have
been his mother. She patronises Art.

She adores Strewelpeter.
May her doting kindness save him.
He is not yet thirty. *Aue!*

Arte & Materia

for Aldo Fregado

What shall we do
  for cotton, for rags
now the forests are burning
  are burning?

What shall we do
  for dancing, for dancing
now the machines
  are turning?

What shall we do
  without horses, no horses
now that our grasses
  are dying, are dying?

Can the wheel turn back?
  Will the wave recede?
Can we rebuild the chapel?
  Will the body break?

Who knows their lines?
  How shall we sing?
Will the graces join in?
  Can we re-arrange it?

What shall we use but
  our eyes, our hands,
letting spirit & nature
  recompose us.

Speaking Through Clouds

for Terrisa J. Mabrey

I

To speak in clay or marble
as figures in clouds mesmerise
dissolve, reassemble, shift their shadows
while a storm gathers far away over
electric on the horizon, you need
to watch the sky for signs.

Gazing, herself a mixture of atoms
bombarding air imploding mind,
a Texas plains child explores
the jutting textures of mountains, mesas, land,
& above all the unpolished
enormousness of sky she's lost in

her head so charged and changed
she turns to her own free-floating
body-in-the-mind in meditation.
Secret, self-contained, continuous
flying like a cloud, she holds
to her femaleness, carving
out of the white marble's cumuli.

She seeks the shaping of her inner sky
as a swimmer, happy in water, voluptuous
in weightlessness, seeks buoyancy's fulcrum.

II

This other form, black marble
hugging the mountain, is male.
Mountains are cloud-catchers—if not
already held, clouds come towards one
or slip down into the sky behind
announcing the birth or death of storms.
Mountains hold land to sky, as *Papa*'s
love for *Rangi* holds earth and heaven.

III

Dancers knitted into a white tube
kick like marble clouds choreographed
to suspend and move on invisible pedestals
a gallery in 3-D round; *Matisse*'s red graces
off the wall, horizontally mobile in a white wind-sock
they hover low, over the planed floor.

These cloud figures floating in relief
are sculpted for your toes, your hands
to prime, to wriggle into. *Touch our coolness*
they say, *we are bubbling domes of water*
touch us and we'll overspill from sky
return to earth, float back to sky.

In Menton after EACLALS at Nice
for Andy Gurr

I'll not forget lunch in the street café
from where we could see Italy,
the border building a bilious yellow
set against the French hill
that became Italy at the building and beyond,
as far as Trieste, round the coast,
past the ecstatic, glinting Mediterranean
where hills hurtle down into headlands
as they do in Wellington or Hong Kong.

You were there and Anna in her flapping
coloured trousers, traipsing towards me
on the sun-lit pavement, to the café,
into my mind's photography where still
I hold you and where Jürgen still smiles,
in the one in which his German face,
all Picasso off-set, describes the African
child tales he teaches, or the one where Dieter
is forever stopped as he charges to the seawall,
changing lenses, to get a telephoto shot of Italy
beyond, the Florence and Venice of dreams.

Firenze, my father's book, on a rainy childhood
Saturday indoors, its sepia photographs
curiously alluring, each with a thin onionskin
protection against mildew and fingerprints.
I gazed uncomprehendingly at page after page
of cornices & cupolas, arches & facades,
astonished buildings could be made so,
not of wood or brick, no corrugated iron;

but how could a book be just of buildings?
Where was the story, the people?

Later, after you'd all gone and we'd visited
the hill villages, St Agnes and Gorbio, where I could
live my life away longing for Italy, the Haleys & I
made an afternoon trip to Ventimiglia, to the market,
a café, to the river, cathedral and the sea.

It was all much grubbier, poorer and differently alive.
The *polizia* wore black not blue, the vegetables
were cheaper, it bustled more. On seeing
an old woman outside an Italian *Oxfam* shop,
perched on the concrete sill in an oblong of sun,
I tried out my best politeness, *"Posso . . .,"*
she scuttled from the sill, gripping her headscarf,
cursing in long strings of words; my self-abasing
*"Mi scusi molto"*s fell on her unhearing ears.
Later a little girl and her pasta-fed Mamma
came to my bench and posed. *"Grazie, mille grazie,"* I said.
It's good to be on top of the world.

Now, time has flung us all far back across the oceans
and we burrow into our wordy cells, the Haleys
writing from England, packing to go home, Anna
in Aarhus, Jürgen and Dieter in *Deutschland* and you
in Reading, reading. And to get again to where we were,
from here in Singapore, I have to think with all my might
of the air that hung so high above us in such sunlight,
that clearly we were part of things

the shape of the bay & the precipitate landscape stuck
with spiky aloes of home that flower once in a hundred years.
We were friends who knew of friends who'd lived there

and so belonged, and like them ate the *plat du jour* at lunch, drinking and laughing, as now and then we paused to gaze across to what might lie beyond the hill that leads to Italy.

Pacific Images

Pohutukawa

for Allen Curnow

    Plenty of space
to think into—
    old pohutukawa
still living
    fledglings scrapping
in his branches
    he grapples
the isthmus of two harbours
    sways to the world
and back
    kicks when it slows
keeps it moving
    on the wind's voice
a wave that speaks
    when it breaks
under that gull
    back-flipping over
into earshot.
    His own sounds
images his own
    knuckles gnarling until
poetry blooms.
    His tongue
lambasts the wind.

Walking A Beach

I

The eye of the mind
is a weather-vane
pointing north to the sun.

Out west, the sea blinks.
The light is not choosy
who sees her—

clarity has no vicious bones
or else she is well-fed
loved and lucky

every time you find her
amidst the facts that slip
now and now

yesterday's thoughts
sandprints walking back and back
and back into the future.

II

Why does this or that
person engage us—who is
found who passed by who come

across who never forgotten?
He-in-my-mind and I
walk re-made and gathering sand;

the beach shelves towards
the oyster-beds; cumulus floats above
that boat-shed on the shore-line.

Water takes everything
with it, perhaps
even the weather-vane

or else what kind of wind
will blow that down or not?
Look, a starfish on the beach.

West Coast Town

The day moon hangs
over a shunted railyard
shanty town.

A jigger's sound
up the track
falls on silence so acute

shapes are cut
from granite
for an echo board.

My voice
bounces back
off the lake's surface,

squawking ducks
sear its glassy skin
sending up shards of spray.

The beach and seagulls
beyond the airstrip
call me.

My father was born here.
I come, a stranger
to the coast.

Is there
no one
to greet me?

To My Father, M.H.K.

My father, who at 82, three years
and twice my age, can still terrify
with an intermittent Napoleonic bark
I went white inside at as a child
a tennis-player with an un-putaway bike
or a huntress become a forlorn rose-bed weeder
ours the normal family sins

now frail and thin, frets against
his uselessness when his eyes cloud up
his breath coming in fits and starts
cleaned through an air-pump three times a day
and then on a good one, perambulates
the lawn with my mother to survey the progress
of a troop of new sweet-peas along the trellis

Captain Kemp who wrote back from the war
thanking my aunt or grannie
for the knitted socks or fruit cake
all the company enjoyed; life's not
much good here—I'm not grousing
it's the same for all the chaps—
and we did see the Pyramids.
On the ship back home he gambled for & won

mother's diamond rings, being quick at cards
& billiards; and now, serving her sherry
on the silver platter, tells again the story
of the belly-dancer who might have been
our mother. I first heard Gershwin & Cole Porter
through the glass door, that let you peep
at sparkling mothers in strapless party dresses

& Morice, hospitality itself at the piano.
Though I always wished him leather-elbowed
tweed-jacketed and wise, with pipe and books
he preferred burning his eartops
in the Coromandel summer sun, up-ended
over the intricacies of the outboard motor's
splutterings & how to get us up on water-skis.

Now, my mother must prepare for him daily, make
soup or the filled bread rolls he likes at lunch
while listening as she reads aloud when the mail
with our letters comes. Daily she consorts
his ups and downs, together they watch t.v.
talk to visitors. Perhaps she wishes he was the kind
who'd read more, so books could give him the things

she knows of, in the blanks.
He says he's not afraid of dying. His dream's
to be put to sea in a boat like ours was
with the bung-hole out and gently to sink down.
This man, my father, is given to our family
to hold close. My mother will read him this
when the next mail comes.

Father's Metamorphosis

He was old and wanted to go.

We all tended to him
wife, sons, daughter
friends. We stroked
his bony forehead
washed him, brushed
his cropped hair
& held his hand. Unlike
anything he'd ever done
like living without memory
he ventured on, each moment
new and groped for.

Images of what he'd been
spun like catherine wheels
in giant circles out of the dark.
He could have been nearly ready
but you never know the time.

He waved a hand, hardly lifted
from the coverlet, when
I had to leave for the airport.
And then the morphine helped him float.
In the plane I knew, as the sun
blitzed the silver wing, that
he'd become the blinding light.

Tropic Night, Port Moresby

Midnight is crickets
a night-jar chuckchucking
a two-stroke twanging
hummed air in its sleep

chuckchuckchucking says
the night-jar I agree

at night everything agrees

sounds fall out of the dark
like birds alighting

the motor-scooter's gone
stroking out twangs

where to where to?
asks the night-owl.

Atalanta

He keeps tossing her
those golden apples
just as she draws level
with his elbow.

Indifferently
she lets them fall.

She wants to range with him
a huntress
and let fly her brilliant arrows

but she's enchanted
by the slow arc
of his arm
and his enticing smile.

Hippomenes on the Waterfront

She went out
looking for him
where he used to be
on the track by the water.

All she heard
were the halyards' hollow thwacks
on distant masts,
yachts at anchor
half a mile from shore;

all she saw
was a fountain
playing to silent houses,
a gallery of empty cars.

How his footsteps drawing near
would make her stumble
how her heart would clang
against the railings of her ribs.

If You're My Friend For Life

If you're my friend for life
don't arrange to meet me
as if your wife's
back's a wall
and the field we'll sit in is small
and golden and strewn with straw don't tempt
me with kindnesses your understanding and far sight don't
let me let you take me into the light
on the other side and leave behind earthly anxiety don't
kiss me as if I give you another horizon.
I can't fit you in on a Wednesday between the train
timetable your wife's burgeoning interest
in computers and my contemplation of hedges.
Your propositions make me feel grubby round the edges.
Go back and tell your wife you love her and life
& rearrange your pattern to include champagne breakfasts
and the moon on Sunday mornings.
Go off now and contemplate new dawnings.
Leave me to play the sibyl.

"Warning Deep Channel off Beach— Bathing Can Be Dangerous At Certain Stages of Tide"

Today at near-high
I walk my solitude along the beach.
Gulls fly up their funnels.
The wind flaps loudly over sea
sluicing through cockles and sand.

Last night, in over my head,
my brain bubbled and boiled
like a hot pool. Now
finding the pulse of things
I'm in at my own depth.

What dervish whirls
without a cloak? What shell
lies loveless on the sand?
What house is unsafe
built on rock?

At Kikowhakarere Bay

A leaf's filigreed skeleton on the beach
silvered by the sun
two paradise ducks, the sound of the sea
these things near me, the given
so accessible.

I've had to come five thousand miles
to be back. Re-made now
I am ubiquitous as the sky or sea
though that figure by the rocks
scribbling in a notebook

is probably me, a traveller
here for a moment, then gone
but always returning like a tide
to possess the beach
& lather the froth of words over the shelly stones.

An
Eastern
Sky

Hong Kong Sounds

Cityscape
skyscrape
Mercedes Benz bus goes
Mongkok sunrise
concrete
block
block
block

hard hat
sunlight
construction site
truck backing
truck backing
truck backing
black pyjama amah
marketing
wax duck
pot luck
tiger balm
dim sum

Star Felly
Day Star Night Star
caterpillar walk on water
Hung Hom
Hung Hom
ho hum
Carlsie Bergie
Susie Wongzie
Hang Seng up down

ding dong deng (xiao ping)
dong
maggie thatcher in beijing
stir-fry
iron dry
nineteen ninety
nineteen ninety
all the sevens
bingo
mah jong
Hong Kong
yum sing!

Hong Kong Headlong From A Motorbike

Free-running eleventh floor eye-level down Pokfulam viaduct
harbour views smack into the visor; three hundred
and fifty dizzy ships shoot out night stars

onto oiled blackness of the sea; giddy with acrobatics
engineering glitters its steel faith in constructing
a planetary city, against earth slip or the ways of water.

The trick is to keep balance whatever hurtles across
the line of sight. Down Queensway, gravity's centre
fires up survival's sense against chance zephyrs side-

swiping at street corners, diesel belching a sudden bumper
a pedestrian stepping out with six flat cooked ducks
sighs from the fish-ball stalls of Wanchai.

Leaning into street-cambers, the city crouches, fish-lens-
eyed, handle-grips tight between fists, she tunnels
under a harbour, six million jam-packing a tenanted sky.

A vision of open road divides the air
where she would ride, the border gates
of a mythical hinterland, the doors to nirvana.

The mountain monks, who laugh at mammon
and guard the passes, do they smile on a rider
revving up for a stunned, crazy attempt to fly?

Street Sleeper, Hong Kong

A street sleeper sits haunched
in the subway entrance, a mat-haired
man with wild fingernails & eyes
turned inwards. Between the tiled
subway floor and his soiled quilt
he has folded newspaper.

His limbs are sticks and twigs.
His body is the tree of life.
He is fruit and flower of a hard city.
He did not make the top branches.
He doesn't drive a gold Rolls
nor does brandy give him

technicolour dreams.
Someone gave him a packet
of shrimp crisps. He picks
them out from the cellophane
one by one, delicate
and savage as a sparrow.

Seascapes, Hong Kong

At Telegraph Bay

Something in the air I must explore:
a summer day, come in winter
dazzling the mica out of these rocks,
making the cold sea delicious,
the craggy islands demure in the mist.

A hydrofoil across Telegraph Bay
shirrs up the waves, the sun
brings my skin out of my clothes,
the sea from under this hat
catches at my eye reflecting and reflecting
off a blue cloth sewn with tiny mirrors.

Junks

I should like it
if the Chinese ancestors
lying here in their bones
in the rubble of a grey-green gully
would let me take down their messages.

I could fashion them
into tiny paper junks
and breathe their sails full
and free them
to the movement of the sea.

Yacht

What do you do?
                I watch the world go.
Where does it go?
                Round the harbour.
What does it see?
                It sees itself.
How do you know?
                I go about
like a yacht.

Bali Rice & Sky

Rice

Lean your ear
down close—
its breath's

as rhythmic as
sloshy snortings
of water buffalo

or seedlings
swishing
a farmer's muddy legs.

Sky

The sky is a poem.
The stars of the plough
hold up the sky.

If every word
were a grain of rice
poets could feed Asia.

Moon Mad

to Li Pai
who tried to hold the moon

You, the night-dancer
try to clutch her.
Her saffron spills
the powder clings
to lily stems.
The fish are golden.
She spins in your hands.
You swallow your mind.

The pond is water-black.

Sky Crosses, Singapore

I have this rectangle of sky to look into
off my balcony ten floors up.
Two pointers go directly to the Southern Cross
(but can I be sure it isn't the false cross
that I'm not tipped over, half-way round
the world from home and seeing askew?)

Well, maybe instead, that's it, off to the left
and those original transversals are the pointers?
No, not bright enough and not enough stars
or dark to see with. Anyway, there's
too much interference from down here
runway lights, heights of building lights

showing you the way to go, you can only see
just in front of you, something's not
quite opened up enough about it all
you can't get any sort of fix through it.
At home, you look straight up and see it
know immediately where you are,

breathe the air, pick up the idiom.
Irina Ratushinskaya says limited human rights
are as impossible as limited breath.
You're free or not, you breathe or don't.
She composed her poems on soap bars,
memorised the lines then washed them off.

They smiled, the women, when led
to solitary, knowing the others,
though weakened by the times before,

would fast for them, knowing freedom
is to know where you stand
in a whole sky, no rectangles.

Appeasement

for Jayanta Mahapatra

To read you is to walk India.
Cows wander in and out of your poems
cripples and beggars lurch along
to sleep, die and be re-born
between steps, between words.

You say you're too much a coward
can't give up enough of self
to do more, must first write
to appease. Lacking faith, you
record the illiterate faithful

whose trance-swallowed tongues
speak only to Lord Shiva.
Their shuffling feet kick up
your muttered mantras
to dance, dustmotes in light.

from Anawhata Sequence

i. At Anawhata

Only our voices and the sea's,
wood-flames talk, the turning
pages of your book. I hear
the stars too, a silver gamelan
tintinnabulating
while the moon in first quarter
sashays through
the cabbage tree.
                                        It's you!
a runaway Asian, writing
in a signal-box perched high
in flax above the Tasman Sea.

At literary conferences, scholars
sweat over files thick with
cultural convergence getting
nowhere close to the bone.

We do it here over chicken stew & wine
two crazies sharing pacific images
in a country neither yours nor mine
but somewhere in the seas between.

vi. Without You

I follow the light fallen from your eyes.
It rages still in the dark.
The bush spirits stare yet cannot harm
despite the hesitation in my step
for I hear the steady sounding of your heart
the assurance of your voice, as you lead
up the spiral path that winds out of chaos.

My most broken, blessed love
how is it you who seared my flesh
& split my bones, illumine me?

viii. Vixen / Iced Grapes

Let me charm the grapes
crushed in my heart
into an airy glass
and carry them out
cold, cold, cold
not opened-to-breathe
red warm, they are
chilled and white
dry ice to my lips
they burn memory's skin.

Delirious drunkard
I watch them, running
my singing finger
round the glass's rim
my body gone blue
my bones tangential
as sticks of crystal
the grapes cold as my bones.

Someone will carve
a figurine of me
place it on a menagerie shelf
to wonder at this
mad bacchanalian.
Shall I ever know why
I sit for millenia
hungry and crouched
made of ice-glass, waiting
for our love to thaw?

Goddesses

Now that we live alone, we women who do
there is much we have time for
whereas he and his
filled the interstices of our days.

Our minds were the gaps we came to
in his absences and wondered at, like
patternings of leaves on a tea-cup's side
or consulted in almanacs or were

what we thought we saw, way up there
between the tree's foliage and the sky
from where we lay below, just woken on a rug
in brief moments, active, alone, alive.

Now he is lost, dead, gone mad or daily
deliberately forgotten, because past had
and impossible to have, we must
re-make our lives and find new ways

to get through the day-to-day;
a job, true friends, little things
to look forward to and above all
seek that lotus plosive in the mind

become Cleopatra, still as clarity
fearless on the Nile of her thoughts
dressed in her own feelings.
These are the secrets of woman's

millennium entombment
as she surfaces, newly discovering,
like a gold-lidded face whose lapis eyes
seeing, can now be seen.

The Other Hemisphere

a poem sequence

The Other Hemisphere

In the other hemisphere Rilke speaks of,
best known to poets and woman whose
unattainable love lives in her mind,
a ghost seen always at his most beautiful,
so gentle he holds her like air, showing
the fullness of heaven by not being there;

deliberately hidden, yet discovered
years after, suddenly in her mind's eye,
on the way to the airport, perhaps,
from the backseat of a taxi, one in a stream
cruising by as shiny and black
as patent leather, seductive as tuxedos,

the thought of him only
rises, flawless as emptiness,
whose wingspan tips the horizon's edges
acknowledging her solitude,
what is left by his absence
filling her sky.

The Dance of Hemispheres

The whole globe's ours—each hemisphere's
a you or I, moulded convex/concave
into a round a sculptor cups in her hands,
that cleaves into a me or you
when the hands part, like seas, receding.

We then re-seek the horizon of our touching,
an equatorial balance to offset us, as
thoughts seek utterance; meanwhile, apart,
silent and obliquely awkward, we roll like
marbles split along the jagged glass eye,

until, space-ships about to dock,
we meet and bow, perform our praying-mantis
courtship dance and lightly spinning, gaily home-in
Escher's doves, one becoming one,
weaving in and out of visibility.

The Gypsy

Suddenly before you, half-turned,
she smiles, this gypsy who leads and leaves,
insouciant anklets like an Indian dancer's,
first overheard, then listened for,
a known footfall, or searched for,
the quick turn of a loved head in a crowd.

This is her, this he/she, this poetry
you follow, leaving the lovers embracing,
gentle snakes coiled on the verandah;
this her, you've jetted the world for,
the sight of her face which comes,
an annunciation, after music and before sleep.

The Phoenix in My Palm

This long line on my palm,
the third line up under the little
finger, the one that matters,
the last, the deepest, cleanest
finest cut, this line is him,
my husbandman, the gardener.

This then is human love, so real
it vanishes illusion and the dance
is visibly laid bare, as to the skin
his touch, my arms remember and hold.
The runes are everywhere and for
always. It was he, first on earth

showed me the phoenix palm, he again
walked through me as if he were
my other self, familiar, easy, there,
walking in the garden or sitting reading
close at hand, under a palm-tree,
reading poems in a low canvas chair.

Self Portrait

I remind myself of Emily Dickinson
locked in the attic of my thoughts
with the casement window flung out open
onto the night air & he who gives me breath

or I'm Heathcliff's girl downed in heather
& the moors pound under me like the purple
galloping surf on a West Coast beach
& romance catches me in the throat again

and I can't unsay it, though I want
the words to tell that this silent well
in me is years strong and filtered
by doubt, gainsaying and turning away.

But who can turn from the truth? It
faces you with the etchings, gouaches
and monoprints in the gallery of your life.
He's the big one down on the farthest wall.

Red Skirt

You're better confined to the page,
a pen and paper love, for if let out,
me in a red skirt & your thick pen

unclipped from a shirt pocket, we wouldn't
hold back; you'd toss off my skirt
and with that pen write all over my skin

till I ran with tattoos of ink and happiness.
What is passion but a red skirt to a pen?
What are poems but the aphrodisiac

of the bull's horns? Picasso knew this,
so too flamenco dancers, and every woman who
stamps under a flounced petticoat with a pretty boot.

In British Columbia once, I watched a stallion
at service. The mare's eyes bolted back
to the whites; strutting, her rump trembled for seed,

her ears flared. He pawed her and foaming
flung himself up and the trees
lunged overhead in the wind, such tall trees

they'd have seeded across the Pacific
so tall they'd have felt the ocean winds
off the Russian steppes. That night

I dreamed of horses plunging the tangy air
their hooves, swaying like branches
their eyes like surf, endlessly rolling.

Marina

Children, like poems, are given
to return us to the seed,
& lovers, prodigal, to re-burst
& scatter it, as the wind
skittering sea foam.

I want to live with him
on that cliff above the beach,
& hear the blowhole heave
in raucous, belching voice
& laugh and hear him laugh,

knowing the child in me
is sown like the best poems
of sea music. I'd name her
Marina, daughter, Oceania.
She'd breathe salt air

& *manuka*, know the horizon
like a spirit-level
& the shape of hills, dark-green,
going-into-black at dusk,
as giant sleeping friends.

I'd show her the side-on rabbit moon
we saw full-faced and equatorial.
I'd tell her I told you I wanted
her then, when I held you,
after years withholding.

Like a great wave she came,
I'll say, from far across

the sea's night, so quiet
in the dark, even the stars
nearly missed its steady unfurling

just as I might have missed
your coming towards me now,
had this poem not been attending.

Suttee

All this love flaming from me,
as if angel voices lit me,
I am dying for,
white song, white pyre,
white piercing the shrieked air.

In my widow's burning robes,
I go, to breathe
only as the sky,
inhaling emptiness; my thoughts,
angeluses of the way's weather

become songs of imagination's heat.
My floating body now is husbanded
by the poems of my life,
my earthen self, white-ashed,
no more to be made wife.

The Mermaid

Compared with other women's loves,
none like you. As day, the night,
I must have you for quietude,
as the moon's peace, the sea.
Rising, her light gives off
fluorescence, like spilling fish.

These years, the rushes of silence.
Where shall I turn?
There is no road.
Only that empty page,
the seamless water & the path
through it, my words divide.